MW01277094

ELDERGYM E-BOOK

Hard Copy Edition

Eldergym e-book

Hard Copy Edition

Copyright © 2010 by Douglas James Schrift MS, PT

All rights reserved. No part of this book may be reproduced or transmitted in any form or by any means without written permission of the author.

www.eldergym.com

ISBN 1453741704

EAN-13 9781453741702

DISCLAIMER

This e-book is intended to provide general information regarding exercises for seniors and the elderly. The content and materials contained in this e-book are provided for general information purposes only and do not constitute medical or other professional advice on any subject matter. Always consult your doctor before undertaking a new exercise program or otherwise increasing your activity level. The author cannot be held responsible for any error, omission, or dated material in this e-book. In no way are there any expressed or implied representations by Eldergym LLC, Douglas J. Schrift, its directors or employees that this content, materials and information constitute or are to be a substitute for medical advice or guidance by a qualified doctor or medical professional regarding specific medical complaints, issues, conditions or diagnoses. Eldergym LLC, Douglas J Schrift, its directors and employees do not accept any responsibility for any loss which may arise from reliance on information contained in this e-book. The author is not liable for any damage or injury or other adverse outcome of applying the information in this e-book in an exercise program carried out independently or under the care a licensed trainer or practitioner. If you have questions concerning the application of the information provided in this e book, consult your doctor.

Please consult your doctor before beginning an exercise program or otherwise increasing your activity level.

Table of Contents

LOWER BODY STRENGTH

Hip Side Extensions	1
Ankle Circles	2
Calf Raises	3
Hip Extension	4
Heel Raises	5
Hip Marching	6
Knee Extensions	7
Hamstring Raises	8
Lunges	9
Sit to Stand	10
Straight Leg Raise	11
Partial Squats	12

UPPER BODY STRENGTH

Bent Over Rows	13
Bicep Curls	14
Diagonal Inward	15
Diagonal Outward	16
Elbow Side Extensions	17
Triceps Kickback	18
Overhead Press	19
Elbow Extension	20
Shoulder Press Lying Down	21
Shoulder Rolls	22
Side Shoulder Raise	23
Upright Rows	24

BACK EXERCISES

Arm Raise On Back   25
Arm Raise On Knees   26
Back Extension   27
Bent Knee Raise   28
Bridging   29
Cat And Camel   30
Crunches   31
Hip Flexion   32
Hip Extensions   33
Pelvic Tilts   34
Eccentric Leg Raise   35
Sit Backs   36

BALANCE EXERCISES

Balancing Wand   37
Body Circles   38
Clock Reach   39
Dynamic Walking   40
Eye Tracking   42
Eye Tracking   43
Stepping Exercise   44
Stepping Exercise   45
Grapevine   46
Heel to Toe   47
Marching   48
Stepping   49
Stepping   50
Single Limb w/ Chair   51
Single Limb w/o Chair   52
Single Limb w/ Arm   53
Staggered Stance   54
Stepping Exercise   55
Stepping Exercise   56

LOWER BODY STRETCH

Ankle Circles   57

Ankle Stretch 58
Back Stretch 59
Calf Stretch 60
Hamstring Stretch 61
Hip Rotation Stretch 62
Inner Thigh Stretch 63
Knee To Chest 64
Standing Quad Stretch 65
Seated Lift 66
Side Hip Stretch 67
Soleus Stretch 68

UPPER BODY STRETCH

Neck Side Stretch 69
Chest Stretch 70
Arm Raises 71
Hand Stretch 72
Neck Exercises 73
Overhead Reach 74
Back Reach 75
Shoulder Circles 76
Shoulder Rolls 77
Shoulder Stretch 78
Triceps Stretch 79
Shoulder And Back Stretch 80

POSTURE EXERCISES

Arm Ups 81
Breathing Seated 82
Standing Breathing 83
Rib lifting 84
Chin Tuck 85
Shoulder Rolls 86
Shoulder Squeeze 87

Seated Spinal Extension   88
Wall Tilts   89

FORMS

Instructions   90
Sample Workout   95
Workout Log   96

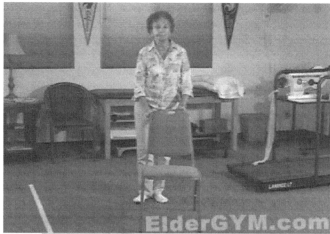

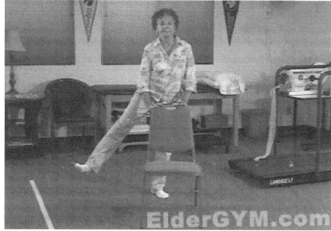

Hip Side Extensions
Step 1

- Stand, using a chair to balance yourself.

Step 2

- Lift your right leg to the side as high as comfortable.
- Return to the starting position, and then repeat 10 times.
- Continue with the left leg.

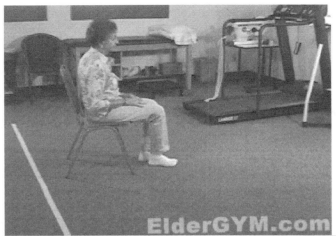

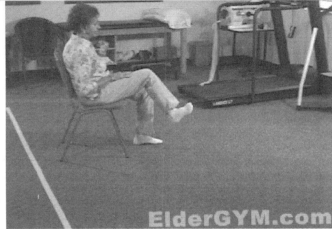

Ankle Circles
Step 1

- Sit in a chair with feet flat on the floor
- Extend your right knee and move your foot in a circle 20 times

Step 2

- Then move in the other direction 20 times
- Repeat with the other ankle

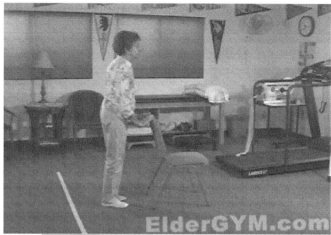

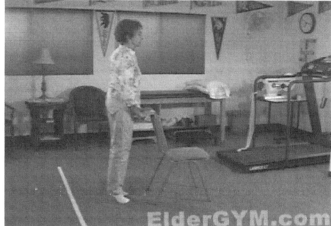

Calf Raises
Step 1

- Stand using a chair to balance yourself.

Step 2

- Rise up on your toes as high as you comfortably can.
- Return to the starting position and repeat 10 times

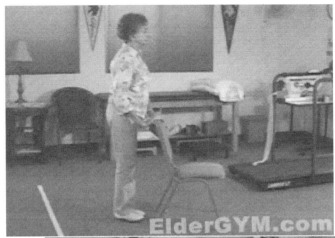

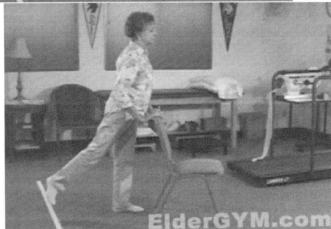

Hip Extension
Step 1

- Stand, using a chair to balance yourself.

Step 2

- Extend your leg backward, keeping your knee straight.
- Return to the start position and repeat 10 times with each leg.

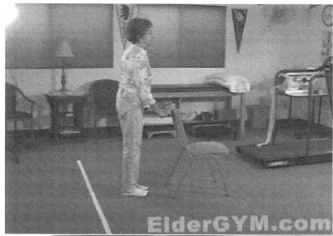

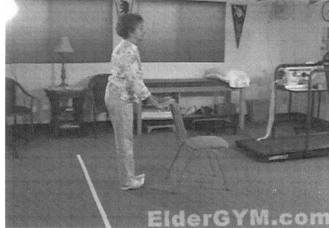

Heel Raises
Step 1

- Stand, using a chair to balance yourself

Step 2

- Rise up on your heels.
- Lower and repeat 10 times.

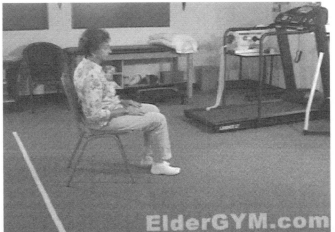

Hip Marching
Step 1

- Sit in a chair with feet flat on the floor.

Step 2

- Lift up your right knee as high as comfortable.
- Lower your leg.
- Alternate lifting your knees for a total of 10 lifts each leg.

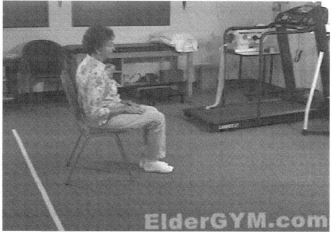

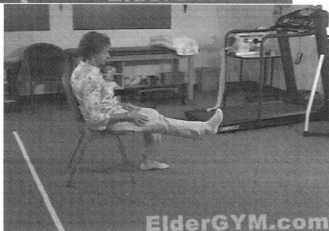

Knee Extensions
Step 1

- Sit in a chair with feet flat on the floor.

Step 2

- Straighten out your right knee and hold for a few seconds.
- Then straighten out your left knee and hold for a few seconds.
- Repeat 10 times on each leg.

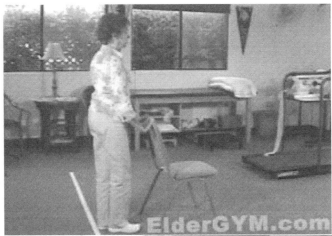

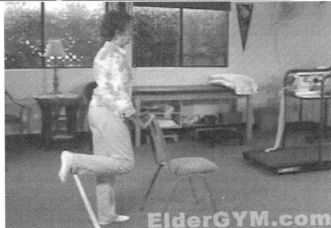

Hamstring Raises
Step 1

- Stand using a chair to balance yourself.

Step 2

- Bend your right knee backward as high as you can.
- Return to the starting position and repeat 10 times.
- Continue with the left leg.

Lunges
Step 1

- Stand with arms at sides or on the hips.
- Keep feet shoulder width apart.

Step 2

- Step forward keeping your trunk vertical.
- Push back up to the starting position.
- Repeat with each leg 10 times.

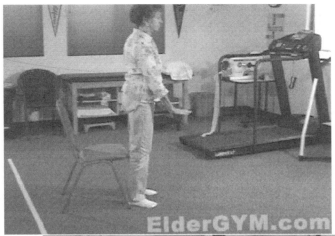

Sit to Stand
Step 1

- Begin by standing with a chair behind you, your knees just in front of the seat.

Step 2

- Lean forward as you bend your knees and lower yourself towards the chair as if attempting to sit.
- Before you touch the chair, pause then stand back up to a full upright position.
- Repeat 10 times.

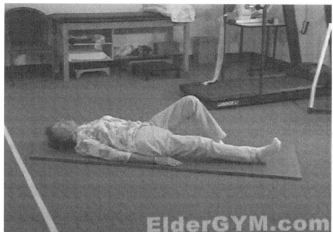

Straight Leg Raise
Step 1

- Lie on your back with one knee bent and one knee straight, toes pointing upward to the ceiling.

Step 2

- Raise your straightened leg to the level of the other bent knee.
- Return to the starting position and repeat with each leg 10 times.

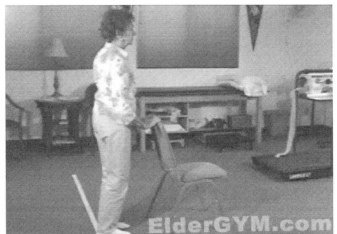

Partial Squats
Step 1

- Stand, using a chair to balance yourself.

Step 2

- Bend your knees as far as comfortable without pain.
- Return to the standing position and repeat 10 times.

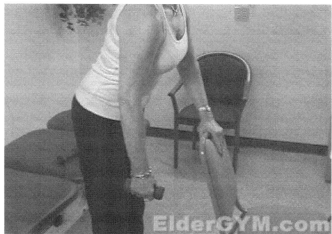

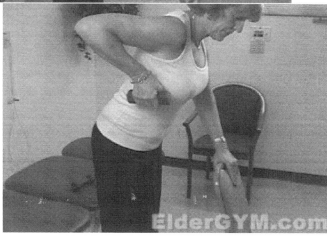

Bent Over Rows
Step 1

- If standing, lean over a table. If sitting, lean over your knee.
- Hold the weight in one arm while supporting yourself on the table or knee with the other arm.

Step 2

- Lift your arm up, raising the elbow to shoulder height.
- Return to the starting position and repeat 10 times.

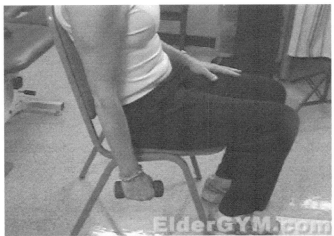

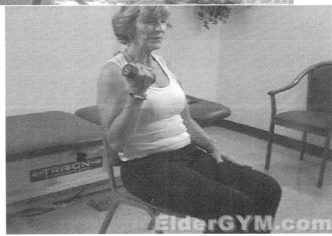

Bicep Curls
Step 1

- Hold the weight in your hand at your side.
- Begin with your shoulders straight and your palm inward.

Step 2

- Bend your elbow toward your shoulder while turning your palm up.
- Return to the start position and repeat 10 times.

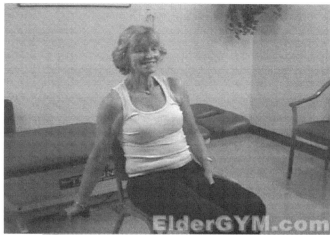

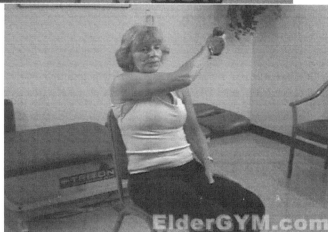

Diagonal Inward
Step 1

- Sit or stand with weight in your hand at your side.
- Hold palm outward.

Step 2

- With palm forward, lift your arm up and across your body to the opposite shoulder.
- Bend the elbow as you bring the arm up and face the palm inward.
- Return to the starting position and repeat 10 times.

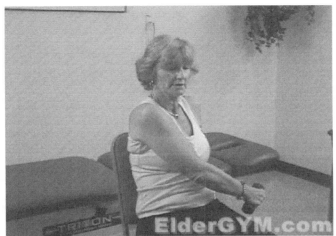

Diagonal Outward
Step 1

- Sit or stand with weight in your hand crossed over to your opposite hip with the palm inward.

Step 2

- Lift your arm up and across your body to the side ending with your palm outward.
- Return to the starting position and repeat 10 times.

Elbow Side Extension
Step 1

- Begin with feet shoulder width apart, feet flat on the floor.
- Holding weights in hands, elbows bent, palms inward on chest.

Step 2

- Straighten arms to the sides.
- Return to the starting position and repeat 10 times.

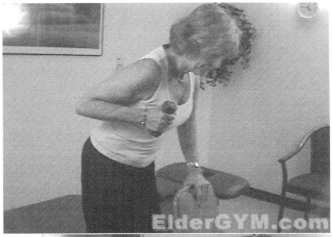

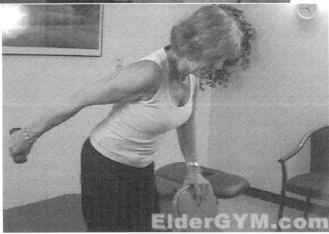

Triceps Kickbacks
Step 1

- Lean over your knee if sitting, or over a chair or table if standing.
- Hold the weight in your hand.

Step 2

- Straighten your elbow behind you as far as comfortable.
- Return to the start position and repeat 10 times.

Overhead Press
Step 1

- Starting with feet shoulder width apart, weights in hand at chest level, palms forward.

Step 2

- Raise arms overhead straight up and out together.
- Lower arms to starting position and repeat 10 times.

Elbow Extension
Step 1

- Hold the weight in your hand.
- Position your arm overhead.

Step 2

- Straighten out your arm toward the ceiling.
- Return to the start position and repeat 10 times.

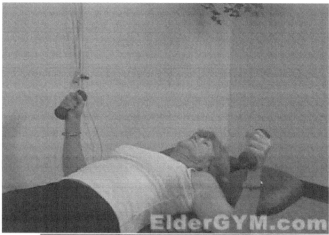

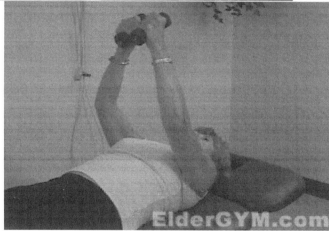

Shoulder Press Lying Down
Step 1

- Lie on your back on your bed or the floor.
- Position head, torso and buttock flat on the surface.
- Hold weights in your hands with your elbows bent at 90 degrees.

Step 2

- Lift arms up toward the ceiling pointing elbows out.
- Return to the starting position and repeat 10 times.

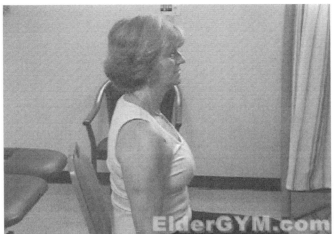

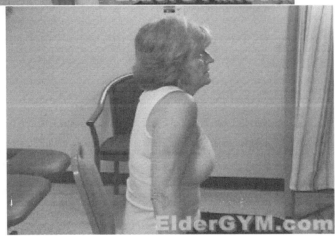

Shoulder Rolls
Step 1

- Stand or sit with weights in hands, arms at side.
- Feet are shoulder width apart.

Step 2

- Raise shoulders upward toward ears, backward and down.
- Return to the starting position and repeat 15 - 20 times.

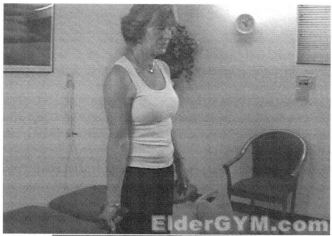

Shoulder Side Raise
Step 1

- Begin with your arm at your side, elbow straight, holding the weight with palm forward.

Step 2

- Raise your arm outward to the side and overhead.
- Return to the starting position and repeat 10 times.

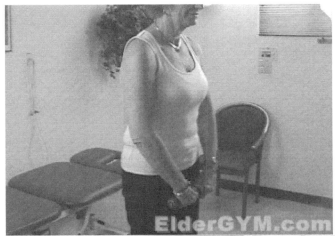

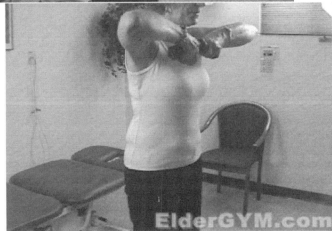

Upright Rows
Step 1

- Stand with weights in hand in front of hips.
- Feet are shoulder width apart.

Step 2

- Lift the weight upward toward your chin, bending your elbows.
- Return to the starting position and repeat 10 times.

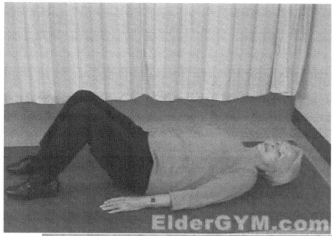

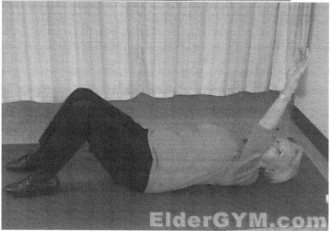

Arm Raise On Back
Step 1

- Lie on your back with your knees bent.
- Keep your low back in neutral and arms at sides.

Step 2

- Lift your right arm off the floor to an upright position.
- Return and repeat 10 times with each arm.

Arm Raise On Knees
Step 1

- Position yourself on your hands and knees.
- Keep your back straight and hips in a neutral position.

Step 2

- Lift up your right arm while keeping your elbow straight.
- Return to the starting position and repeat 10 times with each arm.

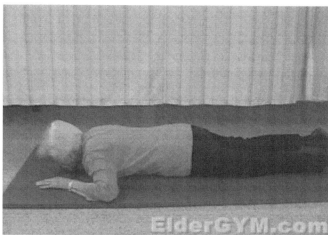

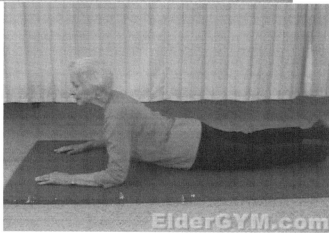

Back Extensions
Step 1

- Begin by lying face down on your bed or the floor with your hands palm down by your face.

Step 2

- Begin to bring your head up and slowly arch your back.
- Push up to your elbows.
- Return to starting position and repeat 10 times.

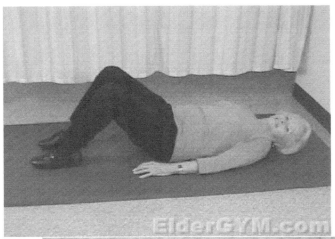

Bent Knee Raise
Step 1

- Lie down on your back with knees bent.
- Tighten up your abdominal muscles.
- Think of your belly button pressing into your spine.

Step 2

- Lift your knees one at a time toward your chest.
- Hold for 5 seconds.
- Return both legs to the floor.
- Repeat 10 times.

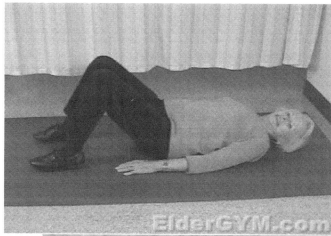

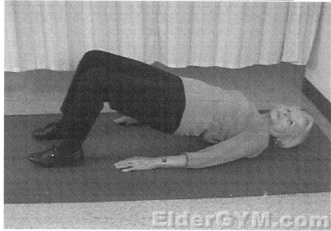

Bridging
Step 1

- Lie down on bed or floor with knees bent.
- Your hips are in neutral.

Step 2

- Lift bottom as high as comfortable off floor.
- Pause, then return to starting position and repeat 10 times.

Cat and Camel
Step 1

- Begin by getting on your hands and knees on your bed or the floor only if you can safely get back up.
- Keep your back in a neutral position.

Step 2

- Round your back up and bring your head down to make the cat arching his back.
- Then reverse by allowing your back to relax forming the valley between the camel's two humps.
- Return to starting position and repeat 10 times.

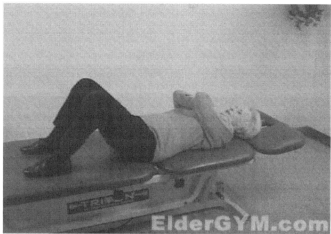

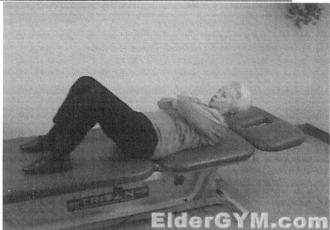

Crunches
Step 1

- Start on back with knees bent and arms on chest.
- Tighten abdominal muscles.

Step 2

- Breathe in, and then exhale as you lift your shoulders off the ground.
- Pause keeping tummy muscles tight.
- Return to starting and repeat 10 times

Hip Flexion
Step 1

- Begin by positioning yourself on your hands and knees.
- Keep your back straight and hips in a neutral position.

Step 2

- Slowly move your hips back, keeping your back as straight as possible.
- Return to the start position and repeat 10 times.

Hip Extensions
Step 1

- Begin by getting on your hands and knees; place your pelvis in a neutral position.

Step 2

- Begin to bring your right leg back, extending it as far as comfortable.
- Return to starting position and repeat 10 times.

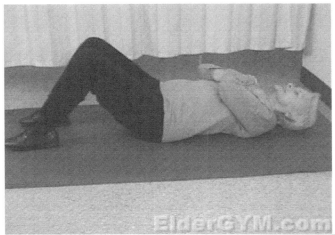

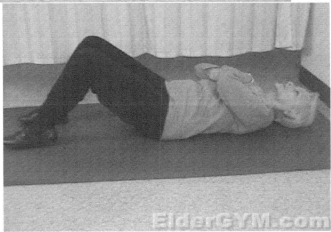

Pelvic Tilts
Step 1

- Lie down on your bed or floor with knees bent.

Step 2

- Tighten your abdominal muscles and begin to press your lower back into the bed or floor.
- Pause, then relax and repeat 10 times.

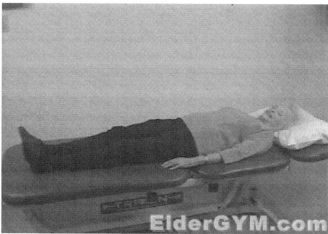

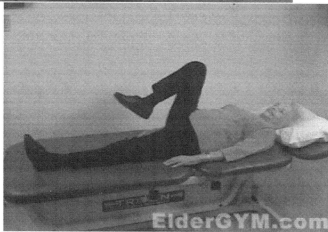

Eccentric Leg Raise
Step 1

- Lie on your back and tighten up your abdominal muscles.

Step 2

- Bring your right knee up toward your chest.
- Keep your left leg on the floor.
- Straighten your right leg and slowly lower to the floor.
- Repeat 10 times with both legs.

Sit Backs
Step 1

- Sit with your knees bent and arms crossed over your chest.

Step 2

- Slowly sit back as far as comfortable.
- Return to the start position and repeat 10 times.

Balancing Wand
Step 1

- Hold a wand in your dominant hand.

Step 2

- Focus at the top of the wand and begin balancing.

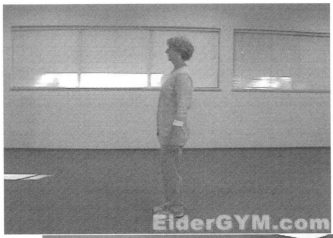

Body Circles
Step 1

- Stand with feet shoulder width apart, hands at sides.

Step 2

- Keeping your body straight, slowly sway in a circle.
- Continue for 1 minute.

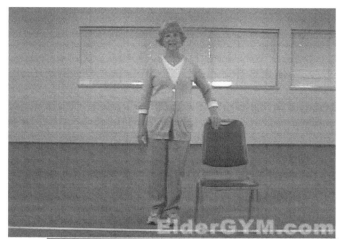

Clock Reach
Step 1

- Begin by holding on to a chair with your left hand.
- Visualize a clock with 12 in front and 6 behind.

Step 2

- Stand on your left leg and bring your right arm to 12 o'clock.
- Then reach to 3 and 6 o'clock.
- Repeat with the other side.

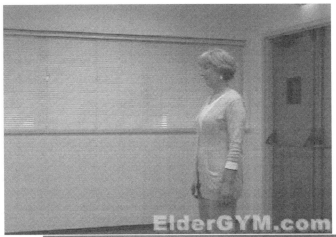

Dynamic Walking
Step 1

- Stand at one end of your living room.

Step 2

- Begin walking while slowly turning your head from left to right.
- Repeat several times.

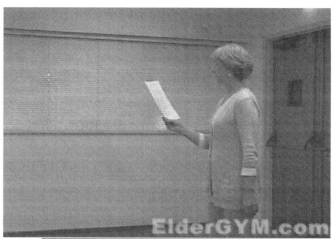

Dynamic Walking With Reading
Step 1

- Now stand with a sheet of paper in your hand,

Step 2

- Begin walking and try turning your head while reading the paper
- Repeat several times.

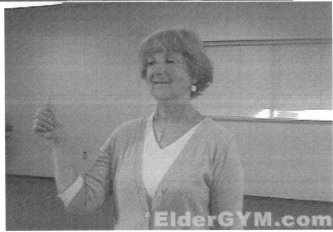

Eye Tracking
Step 1

- Hold your thumb comfortably in front of your face with your elbow bent.

Step 2

- Move your thumb to the right as far as comfortable.
- Then move your thumb to the left as far as comfortable.
- Try not to move your head. Follow with your eyes only.
- Then move your thumb upward, and finally downward

Eye Tracking 2
Step 1

- Now hold your thumb at arms length.

Step 2

- Move your thumb to the right as far as comfortable
- Then move to the left as far as comfortable.
- This time, follow with your eyes and head.
- Move your thumb upward, then downward.

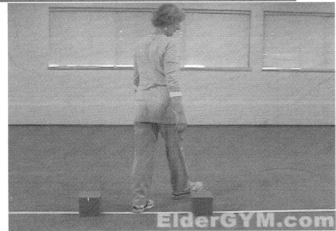

Stepping: Figure 8
Step 1

- Begin with two objects three feet apart.

Step 2

- Begin by walking around each object in a figure of eight pattern.
- Repeat pattern 10 times.

Stepping: Figure 8 in one direction
Step 1

- Begin with two objects 3 feet apart.

Step 2

- This time, keep facing the same direction as you perform the figure eight pattern.

Grapevine
Step 1

- Begin standing with arms at sides, feet together.

Step 2

- Step across in front of your left foot with right leg.
- Continue to step sideways uncrossing the right leg.
- Reverse and cross your right leg behind your left leg.
- Continue to step sideways, uncrossing the left leg.

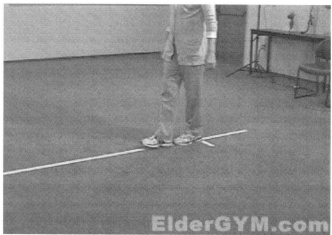

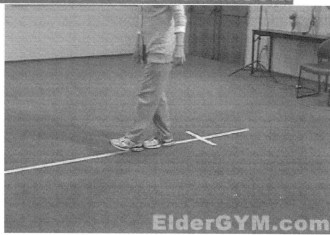

Heel to toe
Step 1

- Begin by standing with one foot in front of the other.

Step 2

- Step forward placing one foot in line with the other.
- Continue to step placing right foot in front of left.

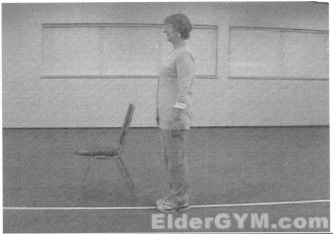

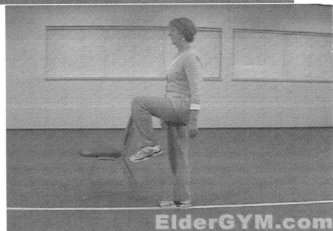

Marching
Step 1

- Stand with arms at sides, feet shoulder width apart.

Step 2

- Raise one knee up as high as comfortable.
- Lower, and then raise the other knee.
- Repeat 20 times.

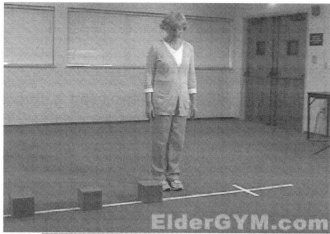

Stepping: Side Stepping Around objects
Step 1

- Begin with two or more soft objects on the floor.
- Space them out 12 to 16 inches apart.
- Stand to one side of the objects.

Step 2

- Begin by stepping forward, then to the side around the object.
- Facing in the same direction, step backward through the objects.
- Repeat this pattern to the last object.

Stepping: Side stepping over object
Step 1

- Begin with 2 objects on floor.
- Space them out 12 to 16 inches apart.

Step 2

- Lift your foot at least 6 inches and side step over the objects.

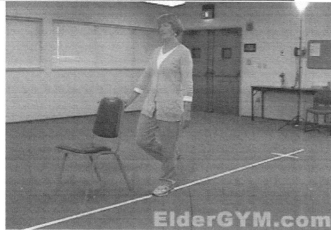

Single Limb Stance with chair
Step 1

- Stand with feet together and arms at sides.

Step 2

- Lift one leg and balance on the other.

Hold for 10 seconds, and then repeat with the other leg.

Single Limb Stance without chair
Step 1

- Stand with feet together and arms at sides.

Step 2

- Lift one leg and balance on the other.
- Hold for 10 seconds, and then repeat with the other leg.

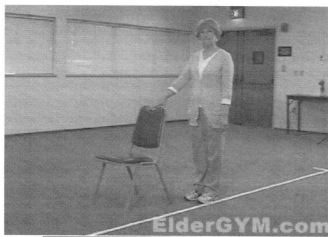

Single Limb Stance with arm
Step 1

- Stand with feet together and arms at sides.
- Hold on to a chair with your right hand for support if needed.

Step 2

- Raise your left arm overhead.
- Then raise your left leg off the floor.
- Hold for 10 seconds.
- Then repeat for the right side.

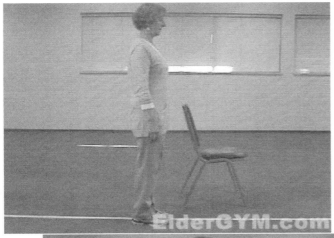

Staggered Stance
Step 1

- Begin with feet together and hands at sides.

Step 2

- Step forward with your right foot.
- Maintain this position for 10 seconds.
- Alternate putting the other foot in front.

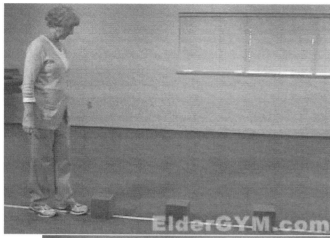

Stepping: Over objects in line with pause between objects
Step 1

- Begin with two or more soft objects on the floor.
- Space them out 12 to 16 inches apart.

Step 2

- Lift your foot at least 6 inches and step over the objects.
- Pause between each object.

Stepping: Over objects in line without pause between objects
Step 1

- Begin with two or more soft objects on the floor.
- Space them out 12 to 16 inches apart.

Step 2

- Lift your foot at least 6 inches and step over the objects.
- Pause between each object.
- Then try stepping over each object without stopping.

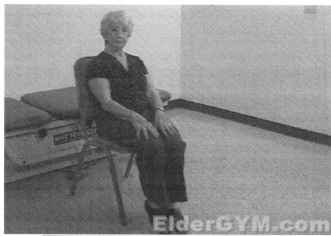

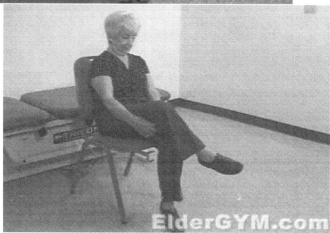

Ankle Circles
Step 1

- Sit comfortably in your chair.

Step 2

- Extend or lightly cross your right leg.
- Circle your right ankle 10 times in each direction.
- Repeat with the other leg.

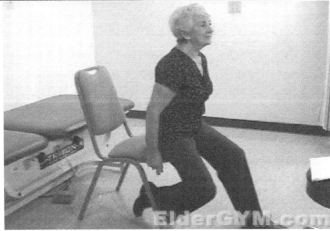

Ankle Stretch
Step 1

- Sit on the front edge of a chair.
- The chair should have an unobstructed underneath section.
- Bring your right foot under the chair.

Step 2

- Gently push down on your foot until a stretch is felt.
- Hold for 20 to 30 seconds.
- Then repeat with the left foot.

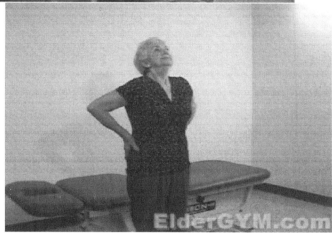

Back Stretch
Step 1

- Stand with your feet shoulder width apart.
- Place hands on your hips with palms against your bottom.
- Inhale through your nose.

Step 2

- Arch your spine backward.
- Hold for 10 seconds, and then repeat 3 times.

Calf Stretch
Step 1

- Stand facing a wall.
- Place your hands on the wall.

Step 2

- Step forward with your right foot.
- Lean your hips toward the wall.
- Keep your back leg straight, heel on the floor.
- Hold position for 20 to 30 seconds.
- Repeat with the other leg.

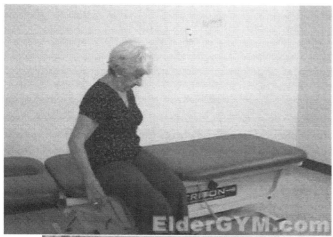

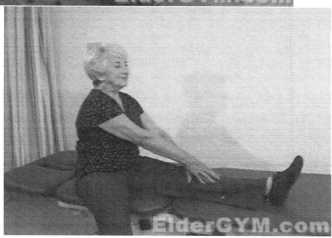

Hamstring Stretch
Step 1

- Select a firm surface to sit upon.

Step 2

- Extend on leg out onto the surface.
- Slowly lean forward.
- Reach for your thigh, knee or ankle.
- Hold for 20 to 30 seconds.
- Repeat with your other leg.

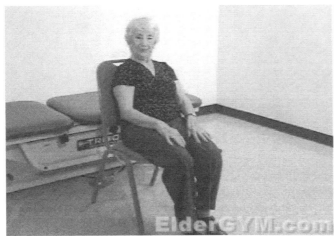

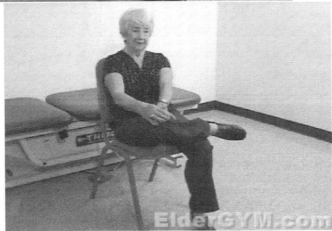

Hip Rotation Stretch
Step 1

- Sit comfortably in your chair.

Step 2

- Cross your right ankle onto your left knee.
- Gently press down on your knee until a stretch is felt.
- Hold for 10 to 20 seconds.
- Repeat with your left leg.

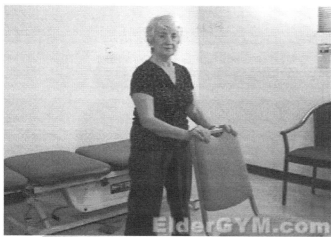

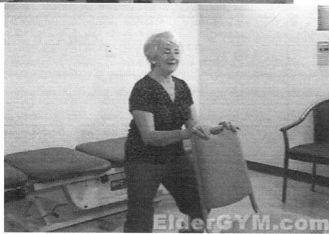

Inner Thigh Stretch
Step 1

- Stand with chair support.
- Bring feet apart as far as comfortable.

Step 2

- Bend knees out to the side and pause.
- Hold for 10 to 20 seconds.
- Then repeat this stretch 2 more times.

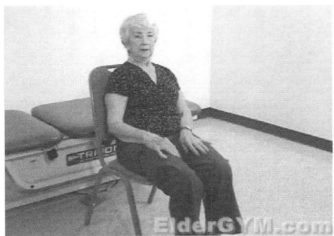

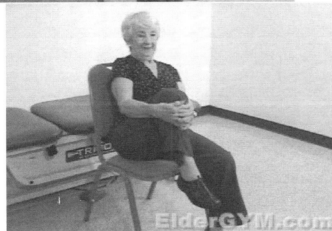

Knee to Chest
Step 1

- Sit comfortably in your chair.

Step 2

- Grasp your right knee.
- Gently pull up toward your chest.
- Hold this position for 10 seconds.
- Repeat with your left leg.

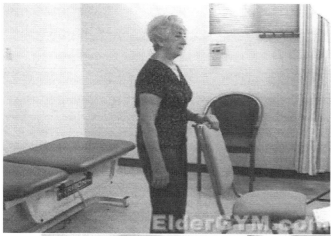

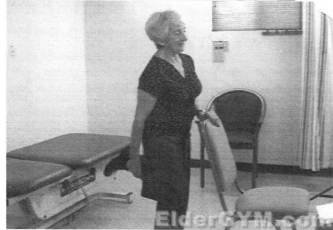

Standing Quad Stretch
Step 1

- Stand with a chair for support.
- Hold on with your left hand.

Step 2

- Bend your right knee.
- Grasp your right ankle.
- Gently pull up toward your bottom.
- Hold for 10 to 20 seconds.
- Then repeat with the other leg.

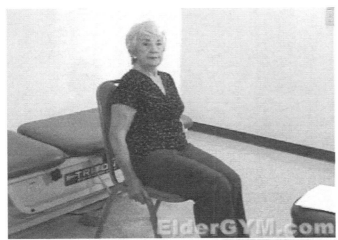

Seated Lift
Step 1

- Sitting in a chair, place your hands on either side for support.

Step 2

- Slowly raise your right hip off the chair.
- Hold for 10 to 20 seconds.
- Then lift your left hip off the chair.

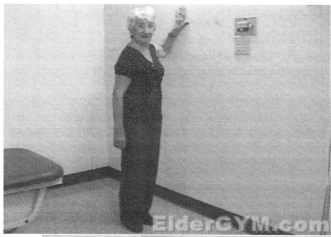

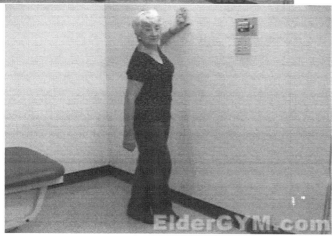

Side Hip Stretch
Step 1

- Stand next to a wall about 12 inches away.
- Your left side facing the wall.

Step 2

- Cross your right leg over your left leg.
- Bring your left hip in toward the wall.
- Hold for 10 to 20 seconds.
- Then repeat crossing your left over your right.
- Bring your right hip in toward the wall.

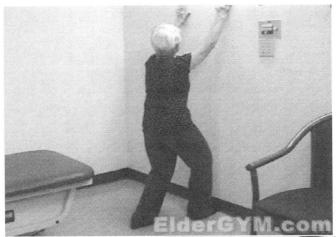

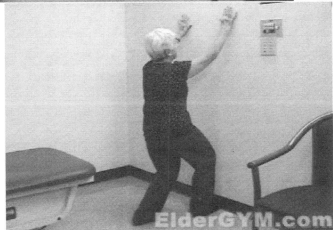

Soleus Stretch
Step 1

- Stand facing a wall.
- Place your right foot in front of the left.
- Place hands on wall for support.

Step 2

- Slowly bend your knees until a stretch is felt.
- Keep your heels on the floor.
- Hold for 10 to 20 seconds.
- Repeat with the left leg in front of right.

Neck Side Stretch
Step 1

- Sit comfortably in your chair.
- Reach your right arm behind your back.

Step 2

- Place your left hand on top of your head.
- Gently tilt your head to the left.
- Hold for 5 seconds.
- Repeat with the other side.

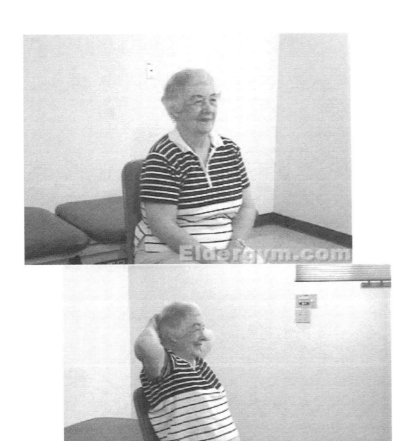

Chest Stretch
Step 1

- Sit comfortably in your chair.

Step 2

- Raise arms and place hands behind your head.
- Breathe in while bringing your neck and shoulders back.
- Hold briefly, then exhale, relax and repeat three more times.

Arm Raise
Step 1

- Begin standing with arms comfortably at sides.
- Relax your shoulders and lift your ribs.

Step 2

- Inhale while you lift both arms overhead.
- Return to the start position and repeat 10 times.

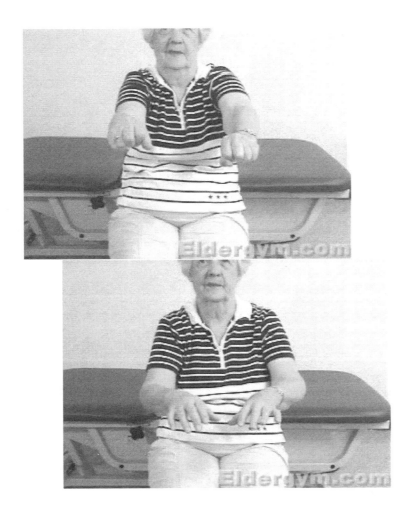

Hand Stretch
Step 1

- Hold your hands out in front with palms down.

Step 2

- Open and close the hand, spreading the fingers apart.
- Repeat 10 times.

Neck Exercise
Step 1

- Sit comfortably in your chair. Look to the right as far as comfortable and hold for 5 seconds.

- Then look to the left as far as comfortable and hold for 5 seconds.
- Bring your right ear to your right shoulder and hold for 5 seconds.
- Then bring your left ear to your left shoulder and hold for 5 seconds.

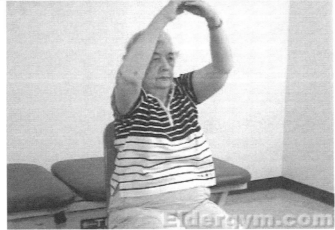

Overhead Reach

Step 1

- Sit comfortably in your chair.
- Inhale and interlace your hands on your lap.

Step 2

- Exhale as you raise your arms overhead.
- Return to the start position and repeat 10 times.

Back Reach
Step 1

- Stand with a chair behind you.
- Inhale as you interlace your hands behind your back.

Step 2

- Exhale and gently move arms backward.
- Pause, then return to the start position and repeat 10 times.

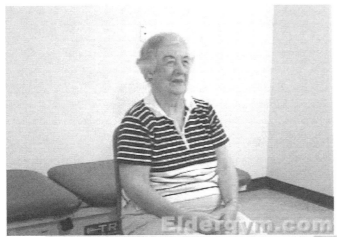

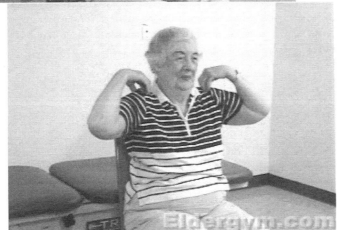

Shoulder Circles
Step 1

- Sit comfortably in your chair.

Step 2

- Place fingertips to your shoulders.
- Circle your shoulders 15 times forward.
- Then circle 15 times backward.

Shoulder Rolls
Step 1

- Sit comfortably in your chair.

Step 2

- Raise your shoulders up, back, then down.
- Relax and repeat 10 times.

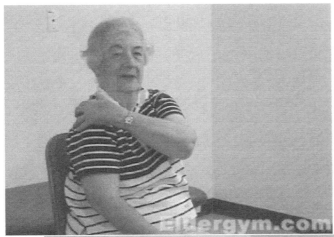

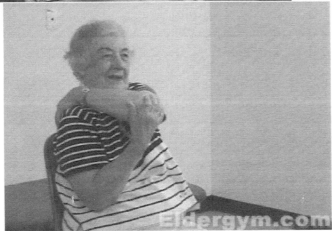

Shoulder Stretch
Step 1

- Bring your left hand up onto your right shoulder.
- Support your elbow with your right hand.

Step 2

- Gently pull left elbow toward right shoulder.
- When a stretch is felt, hold for 10 to 15 seconds.
- Repeat with the other side.
- Gently pull right elbow toward left shoulder.

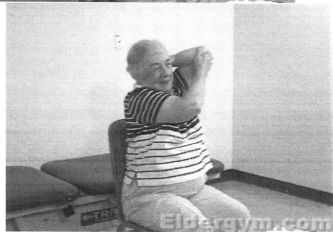

Triceps Stretch

- Sit in a chair while extending your left arm with your palm up.
-] Bring your left arm overhead and pat yourself on the back. For doing a great job of course!
- Bring your right hand to your left elbow.
- Gently press the elbow back until a stretch is felt.
- Hold for 10 to 15 seconds.
- Repeat with the other arm.

Shoulder and Back Stretch

Step 1

- Bring palms together in front of chest.
- Take a breath in through your nose.

Step 2

- Exhale as you bring arms up.
- Straighten arms overhead with palms forward.
- Lower your arms out to the side and back to the starting position.

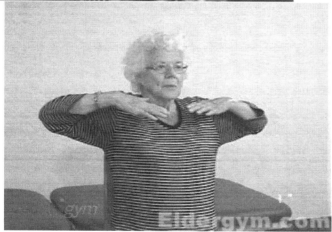

Arm Ups
Step 1

- Sit or stand with arms at sides.
- Maintain a neutral spine.

Step 2

- Breathe in as you raise your elbows to shoulder height.
- Bring your shoulder blades together.
- Return to the starting position and repeat 10 times.

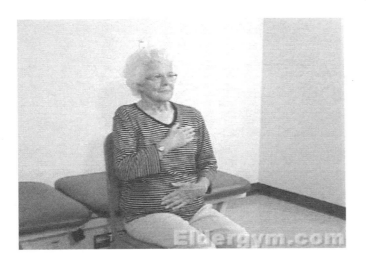

Step 1 Sitting Breathing Exercise

- Sit comfortably in a chair.
- Place your right hand on your chest and your left hand on your belly.
- Inhale so that your right hand rises. This is chest breathing which uses the upper lobes of the lungs.
- Then inhale so that your left hand rises. This is abdominal breathing which uses the lower lobes of the lung. This is the preferred method of breathing in order to maximize the benefits of exercise.

Step 2 Standing Breathing Exercise

- Stand placing both hands on belly.
- Take a deep breath in and expand your belly.
- This is lower lobe deep breathing.

Step 3 Rib lifting Exercise

- Stand with your arms crossed at the wrists in front of your waist.
- Breathe in as you raise your arms overhead.
- Relax and breathe out, lowering your arms. Repeat 10 times.

Chin Tucks
Step 1

- Begin by sitting comfortably in a chair.
- Relax your spine and lift your ribs.

Step 2

- Slowly tuck your chin in, then down to your chest.
- Then continue the exercise by jutting your chin forward.
- Relax and return to a neutral position.

Shoulder Rolls
Step 1

- Sit comfortably in a chair.
- Lift your ribs and relax your spine into a neutral position.

Step 2

- Slowly raise your shoulders up, back and then down.
- Relax your shoulders and repeat 10 times.

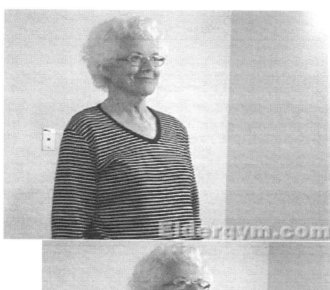

Shoulder Squeeze
Step 1

- Stand with your arms comfortably at your sides.
- Try to find a neutral spine position for your pelvis and mid back.

Step 2

- Begin by bringing your shoulders back, then squeezing your shoulder blades together.
- Relax and return to the resting position. Repeat 10 times.

Seated Spinal Extension
Step 1

- Sit in a chair with arms at sides or on lap.
- Maintain a relaxed spine.

Step 2

- Inhale as you slowly sit up as tall as possible.
- Then exhale slowly as you relax the back and chest.
- Repeat 10 times.

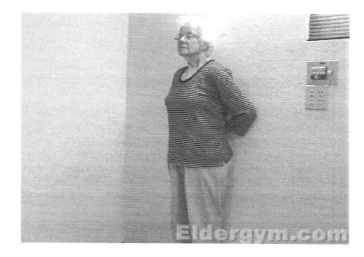

Wall Tilts
Step 1

- Stand with your back against a wall.
- Your feet shoulder width apart, knees are unlocked.

Step 2

- Place one hand behind your back.
- Try to flatten your low back so your hand feels increased pressure.
- Relax and repeat 10 times.

How to use the Exercise Log

- Determine your short term goal. Pick something that is easy to accomplish. These goals should be measurable and realistic goals for us. Take into account your current health status and fitness level. Your goal should be difficult enough to challenge us but also be realistic.
- In our sample the goal is to "be able to tolerate 2 hours of gardening". This is measurable and realistic but challenging.
- Try not to pick something that is not really measurable like "I want more energy". That is not very measurable. But if you can finally begin spending 2 hours in the garden, then you know you have achieved your goal.
- Next determine how many days you can exercise. If you have not been active in a while, try 2 days a week. Then build up from there. Start with 30 minutes if you can.
- Warm up for 10 minutes by walking, riding a stationary bike or simply marching in place.
- Pick two upper body strength, two lower body strength exercises and two back exercises and two balance exercises to start.
- Every week pick a different set of two exercises from each body group.
- Then if you would like to work on your endurance with an aerobic component, try 10 minutes of brisk walking, stationary bike or an aerobics DVD.
- Make sure you cool down with some stretches. Pick three upper body stretch exercises and three lower body stretch exercises.

Before starting, remember to consult with your doctor especially if you have any of the following:

- Chest pain or pain in your left arm and neck
- Any shortness of breath
- A heart condition
- Any bone or joint problems
- If you are currently taking blood pressure or cardiac medications
- Any unexplained dizziness or fainting

Enjoy yourself

Regular physical activity can improve your quality of life in so many ways. Getting injured or discouraged by over exerting yourself will make you exhausted and very likely cause you to discontinue activity.

In order to gain the many benefits of regular exercise, including increased energy, weight loss, improved heart health and strong bones, you must like what you are doing. If swimming feels great, dancing gets your excitement up, bicycling is refreshing then by all means do what your enjoy.

Set Your Goals

Athletes, from runners to weight-lifters, have used exercise logs and goal setting to achieve success.

By recording your progress toward your goals you will gain perspective and be able to answer the question I get most often...How do I know if I'm getting stronger?

Let's say you want to be able to get out in the yard and garden for two hours. That is your *short term goal*. You decide to begin with a walking and weight lifting program.

- On your first day of exercise you can walk for 5 minutes at a brisk pace and lift a five pound weight 10 times before getting tired.

- You then continue to exercise and record what you are able to do at least weekly in your journal.

- At the end of 6 weeks you have increased your walking time to 20 minutes and lifting capacity to eight pounds 10 times.

Wow! Now you can answer the question yourself...
I AM getting stronger! And ultimately 2 hours in the garden is easily accomplished. (As long as the weather holds!)

Equipment

Setting up an exercises for the elderly program at home doesn't require a lot of investment in equipment. Unless you really have your heart set on that new all purpose gym from Sears!

More than likely though it will be in your garage serving as a clothes hanger in a few short months. All you really need is a sturdy armless dining room or kitchen chair and a few weights.

A 2 pound, 3 pound, 5 pound and 8 pound will likely serve the needs of most older adult exercisers. Make sure you have athletic type shoes that offer good support such as walking or running shoes. Your clothing should also be comfortable and loose fitting.

Schedule Your Exercise

How do ants make an ant hill so tall? They consistently add one grain of sand at a time. It's the little bit you do every day that will over time increase your strength and endurance.

To be consistent requires taking a good look at your day and week. What days will I most likely be able to fit in exercise? What time of day would be best?

The longer you are faithful to the schedule the easier it will be to stick to the exercise program.

How hard should I exercise?

Your workout should be intense enough to make your heart beat faster and your breathing to increase but not so high as to over stress your system. This is your training zone. Try to work out in this range to get the most benefit out of your exercise.

Below you will find three good ways of monitoring your intensity level and finding your training zone. Pick one that will work for you and your situation.

Method 1: Maximum Heart rate:

- A good range for the typical senior exerciser is between 60% to 70% of your maximum heart rate.
- To find your maximum heart rate, subtract your age from the number 220.
- This is your maximum predicted heart rate for one minute.
- For example, let's say you are 75 years old.
- 220 - 75 = 145 beats per minute.
- 145 is the maximum your heart can beat in a minute.
- 60% of 145 = 87 beats per minute (low end of range)
- 70% of 145 = 101 beats per minute (high end of range)
- Therefore your training zone is 87 to 101 beats per minute.

Since it is impractical to count your pulse for 60 seconds you can take a ten second count and multiply by six. A 75 year old man needs to exercise between 14 and 17 beats when counting for 10 seconds.

- 14 beats in 10 seconds is your low range.
- 17 beats in 10 seconds is your higher range.

Review the 10 second counts so that you don't have to do math in your head while exercising. Slow down for the pulse count but keep your legs moving.

It is usually better to take your pulse at your wrist (radial artery) instead of your neck (carotid artery). It is possible to press too hard on the carotid artery which could cause slowing of the pulse. It is a good idea to take your pulse:

- Take your pulse at approximately 5 minutes into the exercise.
- Take your pulse again at approximately 10 minutes into your endurance exercise or after the hardest part.

- Take your pulse just after your cool-down.

Method 2: **Rate of Perceived Exertion:**

An easier method is to just rate your feeling of how hard you are working on the 6 to 20 scale. This is called the Borg Scale of Perceived Exertion.

- 6 No exertion at all
- 7 Extremely light
- 8
- 9 Very light
- 10
- 11 Light
- 12
- 13 Somewhat hard   "TRAINING RANGE"
- 14
- 15 Hard
- 16
- 17 Very hard
- 18
- 19 Extremely hard
- 20 Maximal exertion

For most older adult exercisers, you can work in the "somewhat hard" range which is 12 to 14.

- *Method 3:* **Talk Test:**

   You should be able to speak in your normal voice and tone during your exercise session. If you are out of breath and are unable to speak regularly, then you need to lower your intensity level by slowing down.

How long should I exercise?
You don't need to work hard for a long time to gain benefit from exercise. You can exercise 10 minutes in the morning and 10 minutes at night.

Begin with 20 to 30 minutes of exercise to start. Build up to an hour if you are able.

How often should I exercise?
Try working out 2 days a week to start. Then increase a day or two as you get comfortable with exercising. 3 to 5 days a week is usually well tolerated. Don't work the same muscle group on consecutive days.

Don't exercise beyond 5 days a week unless you receive personal instruction and a professionally designed program.

How much weight should I use?

Arms: Try starting with 2 pounds. This is usually tolerated by most seniors. Women can safely train up to 5 pounds and men can safely train up to 8 pounds for the upper body.

Legs: Our legs are fairly heavy and may not require additional weight. If you choose to use weights for the legs, use ankle weights. Seniors can usually safely start with 1 pound ankle weights. Work up to 3 pounds if you are tolerating the weight well and can do at least 15 to 20 repetitions comfortably.

What are some general safety guidelines for exercise for the elderly?

1. Remember that with age, sudden intense exercise may be a challenge for your heart. Try to prepare your muscles with a 10 minute warm-up before exercising.

2. Also, quickly stopping during a workout may cause blood to pool in your legs, increasing the strain on your heart. That is why a 10 minute cool-down session is important.

3. Monitor yourself for overexertion which is indicated by shortness of breath, nausea, dizziness or getting that shaky feeling. Make sure you listen to your body!

4. Make sure you increase your activity level gradually. Only add 5 to 10% increase to any workout.

5. Think "posture" as much as you can during your workout. Good posture will help protect your joints and prevent any unnecessary injuries.

6. Practice good breathing. Never hold your breath. Try to breathe in through the nose and out the mouth.

7. Train at the Goldie Locks intensity. Not too high and not too low. We want your heart to make improvements in its aerobic fitness which requires training in the 50% to 75% range of your maximum heart rate.

Remember, exercises for the elderly training will only show benefits if it is done regularly with the correct duration, frequency, and intensity.

Eldergym® Sample Log *Aug 26, '11*

SHORT TERM GOAL: *To be able to tolerate 1 hour of gardening 6 weeks from now*

	DAY 1	DAY 2	DAY 3
WARM-UP	Min. 10	Min. 10	Min. 10
	Stationary Bike	*Walking around block*	*Stationary Bike*
EXERCISE	Wt/Sets/Rep	Wt/Sets/Rep	Wt/Sets/Reps
1. Chest Stretch (Page 70)	0-lb/1/x3	0-lb/1/x3	0-lb/1/x3
2. Arm Raise (Page 71)	0-lb/1/x10	0-lb/1/x10	0-lb/2/x10
3. Neck Stretch (Page 73)	5 Sec	5 Sec	5 Sec
4. Overhead Press (Page 19)	3-lb/1/x10	3-lb/1/x10	3-lb/2/x10
5. Upright Row (Page 24)	3-lb/1/x10	3-lb/1/x10	3-lb/2/x10
6. Biceps Curls (Page 14)	3-lb/1/x10	3-lb/1/x10	3-lb/2/x10
7. Triceps Kickback (Page 18)	3-lb/1/x10	3-lb/1/x10	3-lb/2/x10
8. Elbow Extensions (Page 20)	3-lb/1/x10	3-lb/1/x10	3-lb/2/x10
9. Chest Press (Page 21)	3-lb/1/x10	3-lb/1/x10	3-lb/2/x10
10. Knee Extensions (Page 7)	0/1/x10	0/1/x10	0/2/x10
11. Sit to Stands (Page 10)	0/1/x10	0/1/x10	0/2/x10
12. Hip Side Extensions (Page 4)	0/1/x10	0/1/x10	0/2/x10
13. Lunges (Page 9)	0/1/x10	0/1/x10	0/2/x10
14. Standing Calf Raises (Page 3)	0/1/x10	0/1/x10	0/2/x10
15. Partial Squats (Page 12)	0/1/x10	0/1/x10	0/2/x10
16. Calf Stretch (Page 60)	30 Sec	30 Sec	30 Sec
17. Hamstring Stretch (Page 61)	30 Sec	30 Sec	30 Sec
AEROBICS	Min. 10	Min. 12	Min. 15
	Treadmill	*Treadmill*	*Treadmill*
Heart Rate Range = 90 - 105 bpm	90 bpm	92 bpm	94 bpm
COOL-DOWN	Min. 10	Min. 10	Min. 10
	Walking	*Walking*	*Walking*

Eldergym® Exercise Log ___/___/___

SHORT TERM GOAL:			
	DAY 1	DAY 2	DAY 3
WARM-UP	Min.	Min.	Min.
EXERCISE	Wt/Sets/Rep	Wt/Sets/Rep	Wt/Sets/Reps
1.			
2.			
3.			
4.			
5.			
6.			
7.			
8.			
9.			
10.			
11.			
12.			
13.			
14.			
15.			
16.			
17.			
AEROBICS	Min.	Min.	Min.
Heart Rate Range =			
COOL-DOWN	Min.	Min.	Min.

8956106R0

Made in the USA
Charleston, SC
31 July 2011